EXPEDITION AUSTIN

A Kid's Guide to the Weirdest Town in Texas

words by

Jill Coody Smits

illustrations by

Virginia Shurgar Hassell

ISBN 978-0990831518

Look up!

Otherwise, you might miss some of the weirdest stuff on Expedition Austin. Turn to page 74 to learn more about the Cathedral of Junk, where you'll find this dreamy skylight.

For my co-editor, Stella, and co-everything, Jasper.
And for Austin, the awesomest hometown on the planet. — JCS

For Madeleine, Sophie and Whit — my Viking playmates —
and Luke who brought us home to Austin — VSH

Jill Coody Smits www.blueseedcommunications.com
Virginia Shurgar Hassell www.bigstarcreative.com/blog

AUSTIN

FUN FACTS

Population: 931,830 (2015)

Area: 271.8 square miles

Size Prize: Austin is the 11th largest city in the United States

Weather: More than 300 sunny days every year

Famous Food: Tacos, BBQ

Cool Critters: Coyotes, bobcats,
bats, armadillos, deer, owls

ENCHANTED ROCK

BLUE HOLE

LADY BIRD
JOHNSON
WILDFLOWER
CENTER

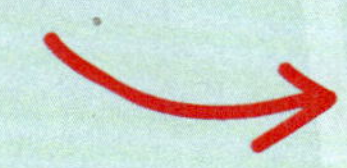

AUSTIN
RODEO
LADY BIRD LAKE
ZILKER
PARK
BUTLER
PARK
SOUTH
CONGRESS
FORMULA 1

TABLE OF CONTENTS

READY, SET...EXPEDITION AUSTIN!

Woohoo! You've got yourself a fun-filled, kid-friendly guide to the weirdest town in Texas! It's packed with cool pools, awesome activities and mind-blowing museums, but you'll want to read these useful tidbits before starting your adventure.

FUN FACTS

» Each place highlighted in the book comes with a few facts that are fun to know. Read and learn, then take the quiz in the back of the book. Don't worry, you won't be graded!

THE LOWDOWN

» This info is super useful for your parents, who will need to know things like addresses, business hours and where to park (and buy ice cream).

BE YOURSELF

» When you're out and about in Austin, the weirder you are, the better! Go out, have fun, and BE WEIRD. Just look at these crazy kids!

MISSIONS

Since you're on an *expedition*, you must complete one mission at each place you visit—36 tasks in all! Give yourself a pat on the back and color in the "thumbs up" icon when you've completed it.

#EXPEDITIONAUSTIN

» If you or your parents socialize on Instagram, ask them to show you #ExpeditionAustin to see other kids' adventures and share your own. Visit expeditionaustin.com for all kinds of cool ideas!

GREETINGS FROM
AUSTIN
TEXAS

SPLASH!

JUMP IN A BLUE-GREEN POOL,
CLIMB SOME ROCKY HILLS.
HOLD YOUR NOSE, GET COOL.
(DON'T FORGET TO PACK YOUR GILLS.)

SPLASH MISSION #1   FIND THE PHILOSOPHER'S ROCK NEAR THE MAIN ENTRANCE.
TELL YOUR PARENTS WHAT YOU THINK THE FRIENDS ARE DOING AND WHY YOU THINK
THE STATUE WAS CHOSEN FOR BARTON SPRINGS.

BARTON SPRINGS POOL

Cannonbaaaaaaall! Smack dab in the middle of Zilker Park, beautiful Barton Springs Pool is an awesome place to cool off on a hot Austin day. For one thing, it is three acres huge! Also, you can have all kinds of fun, like slipping and sliding on the natural rock bottom, searching for fish and turtles in deeper water or doing tricks on the diving board. When you're done swimming and relaxing on the big grassy hill, take your parents to get something cool to drink at the café, then hit the nearby playground or ride around the park on the Zilker Zephyr mini-train—you might even see some dogs playing Frisbee!

Color YOUR OWN Barton Springs salamander (Eurycea sosorum)

FUN FACTS

» The clear water is fed by four underground springs, which means it is a chilly 68 degrees all the time. Brrrr!

» The pool is a protected habitat, and the only place on the planet where you can see the Barton Springs salamander. (Hint: Look for these endangered, hard-to-find amphibians near Main Spring, just upstream from the diving board.)

» Although the pool is named for William "Uncle Billy" Barton, who lived nearby in the 1800s, archaeologists tell us that Native Americans used the springs long before that.

THE LOWDOWN

» GEAR   Swimsuit, goggles, towel, good book, noodle or small float, sunscreen.

» TELL YOUR PARENTS   You'll need cash for entry ($1/$3 for resident kids/adults; $3/$8 for non-residents) as well as for snacks and a ride on the Zephyr. No food is allowed in the pool area.

» KNOW BEFORE YOU GO   Open in summer from 8AM to 9PM, Barton Springs is located at 2201 Barton Springs Rd. There are parking lots at the main entrance and across the street from Umlauf Sculpture Garden on Robert E. Lee Rd. The springs are open year round, but closed on Thursdays for maintenance. (512-867-3080)

CAMPBELL'S HOLE

With rocks to scramble down, frogs to find and woodsy bridges to cross, the hike down to Campbell's Hole is just as much fun as swimming in it. At the end of that 15-minute walk, you're sure to find some splashy good fun at one of the most popular spots on the Barton Creek Greenbelt. Just what kind of fun, though, depends on how rainy it's been in Austin. Maybe you'll find a raging river, perfect for sending stick boats shooting down the rapids. Or, you might find a crystal clear creek, flowing just fast enough to body surf in a few inches of water. If you're here in the heart of summer, though, you may get to rock hop across dry waterfalls and hunt for tadpoles in shallow limestone pools. The only guarantees are that no two visits are the same, and all visits are awesome.

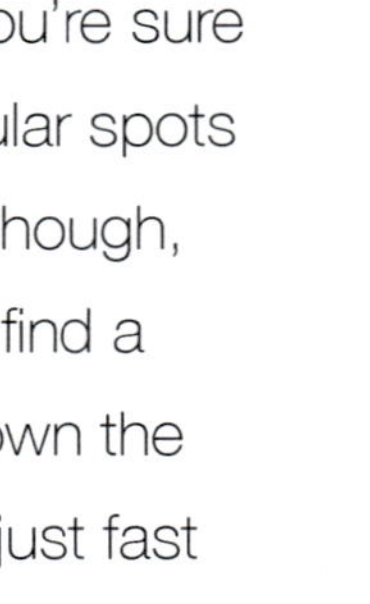

FUN FACTS

» The limestone beds you'll stand on were deposited here about 100 million years ago!

» You might see some fluttering butterflies on your walk around Campbell's Hole—there are 130 species in this section of the greenbelt.

THE LOWDOWN

» GEAR   Swimsuit or clothes that can get wet, water shoes, water bottle, picnic snack.

» TELL YOUR PARENTS   Visit early! Because it's so close to downtown Austin, Campbell's Hole can get very busy, especially when it's hot and the water's flowing.

» KNOW BEFORE YOU GO   There are two (free) entrances to Campbell's Hole, including one located at 2010 Home Dale Dr. Lots of people walk their dogs off-leash near this special place.

SPLASH MISSION #2   TRY AND SPOT SOME BALANCED ROCK TOWERS ALONG THE LIMESTONE BANKS AND FOCUS ON BUILDING A TOWER OF YOUR OWN. DOES IT MAKE YOU FEEL PEACEFUL?

SPLASH MISSION #3   WANDER OVER TO THE DEEP END OF DEEP EDDY POOL, SHOW
OFF YOUR VERY BEST RACING DIVE AND SWIM A LAP.
18

DEEP EDDY POOL

We don't want to brag, but Austin swimming pools are the best in the country. Take Deep Eddy Pool, for instance. While it may look like an average neighborhood pool at first, it is actually a 600,000-gallon hole of spring-fed watery fun unlike any other. For one thing, it will stay an always-perfect 65-75 degrees even on scorching hot days. For two, it overlooks Lady Bird Lake. For three, there is always a fun cast of characters to make friends with. For four, you can watch your favorite movies while floating in the pool on hot summer Saturdays. And, for five, it's one of only a handful of places where you can get a tiny but perfect cup of Jim-Jim's water ice.

FUN FACTS

» Established in 1915, Deep Eddy is the oldest swimming pool in Texas, and used to be part of a big resort where you could camp or stay in a cabin.

» During that time, a woman named Lorena would entertain guests by diving from a 50-foot-high platform into the pool...while riding on a horse. (Poor horse!)

THE LOWDOWN

» GEAR   Swimsuit, goggles, small float, towel, cash for entry and snacks.

» TELL YOUR PARENTS   Please buy me a Jim-Jim's water ice!

» KNOW BEFORE YOU GO   Located at 401 Deep Eddy Dr., the pool is open for recreational swim from 10AM to 8PM on weekdays and 8AM to 8PM on weekends. There is a parking lot, and (cash only) entry is $1/$3 for resident kids/adults and $3/$8 for non-residents. Check deepeddy.org for summer movie times. (512-472-8546)

PADDLE & RIDE

PEDAL, OAR, WALK OR ROLL:
SO MANY WAYS TO MAKE THE TRIP WITH ZIP.
PICK YOUR RIDE, SET A GOAL,
THEN LET HER RIP.

AROUND LADY BIRD LAKE

There are lots of adventures to choose from on the 10-mile hike-and-bike trail wrapping around Lady Bird Lake. If you're feeling fierce, ride your bike in a huge lap and see it all. Or, choose from several small sections along the way. Hop on at the Ann W. Richards Congress Avenue Bridge if you want to hear, see and *smell* a bat colony, feel what it's like to bike on water at the nearby boardwalk and gaze up at a huge statue of Stevie Ray Vaughan, Austin's most famous guitar hero. Or, try the Lamar Boulevard pedestrian bridge if you want to scooter across the lake or walk to Zilker Park, where you can have a picnic, watch a Quidditch match and climb on a rock island. Whichever adventure you do choose, it's sure to be fun.

FUN FACTS

» Ann W. Richards was the first elected female governor of Texas. Today, there are many more women governors in the U.S., but there were only a few in 1990. She was quite a character and a lifelong advocate for equality and women's rights.

» From March to November, 1.5 million Mexican free-tailed bats roost under the Congress Avenue Bridge. You can hear them all the time, and watch them fly off to find their insect dinner each night around sunset.

» Stevie Ray Vaughan started playing guitar when he was 7 years old. He died way too young at age 35, and is considered one of the best blues guitarists who ever lived.

THE LOWDOWN

» GEAR   Bike or skates, helmet, water bottle, picnic blanket, snacks.

» TELL YOUR PARENTS   You can bike down to the trail or drive and park along Cesar Chavez St. or Riverside Dr. A large free lot is on Lou Neff Rd. in Zilker Park. Rent bikes from a nearby place like Bicycle Sport Shop (bicyclesportshop.com) or Barton Springs Bike Rental (bartonspringsbikerental.com)

» KNOW BEFORE YOU GO   Only parts of the trail are paved and good for skating. Also, if you want to see the bats fly away, check and see what time the sun is setting. In the middle of summer, it can be pretty late.

PADDLE & RIDE MISSION #1   FIND THE STATUE OF STEVIE RAY VAUGHAN AND
TAKE A PHOTO. ASK AN ADULT TO PLAY HIS SONG "MARY HAD A LITTLE LAMB."
ANSWER TWO QUESTIONS: WHY IS HIS SHADOW IN THE STATUE SO LONG? WHY DO
YOU LIKE OR DISLIKE HIS SONG?

PRETEND YOU'RE A FISH IN THE WATER. PICK THREE PLACES YOU'D LIKE TO HANG OUT WITH YOUR FISH PALS, AND STEER YOUR CRUISER THERE. MAKE YOUR VERY BEST FISH FACE UPON ARRIVAL.

ON LADY BIRD LAKE

While an adventure *around* Lady Bird Lake is awesome, an adventure *on* the lake might be a tiny bit better. First, you get to choose a cruiser. You can share a kayak or canoe with someone who can help you row, or get your own stand up paddleboard if you have good balance, a lot of energy and very strong arms. Once you're out there floating, there's plenty of exploring to do. See what happens when you stop paddling, and the wind carries you along with it. Be sure and paddle close to the shore, as you are certain to see turtles sunning themselves on logs. Finally, take a look at downtown Austin and all of the people exercising on trails and bridges overhead. Do you like your fish-eye view?

It's a cluster of canoes! Color them in, and write your name on the one you want to take out.

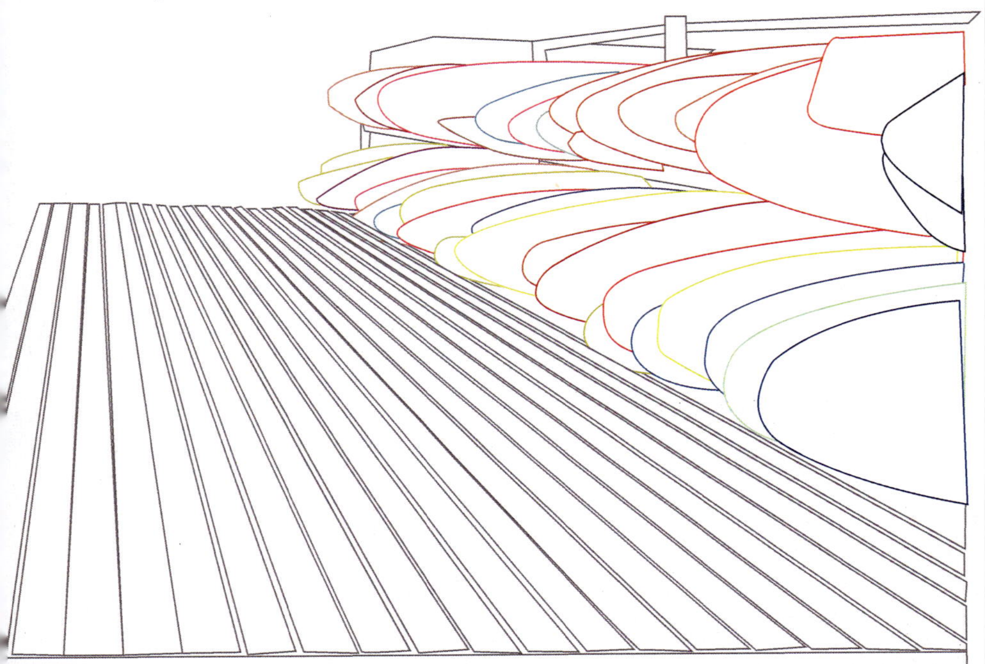

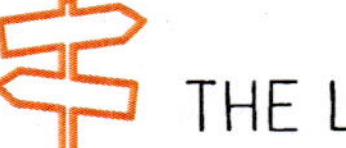 FUN FACTS

» Lady Bird Lake used to be called "Town Lake," even though it isn't really a lake. It's actually a dammed segment of the Colorado River.

» There's great bird watching on the lake. Keep your eyes peeled for grebes, loons, pelicans, cormorants, herons, egrets, vultures, ducks, hawks, rails, plovers, sandpipers, gulls, terns, titmice, chickadees, wrens, hummingbirds, woodpeckers…the list goes on and on!

» The Pac-Man graffiti art you might see while paddling near the railroad bridge has been removed then repainted numerous times.

THE LOWDOWN

» GEAR   Swimsuit or clothes that can get wet, life jacket, and a bag to store things that you don't want to drop in the lake.

» TELL YOUR PARENTS   Check and see which way the wind is blowing. It's much harder to paddle against the wind, and you might want to go that direction first.

» KNOW BEFORE YOU GO   There are several places to rent cruisers, and they all provide life jackets. Rowing Dock is at 2418 Stratford Dr. Zilker Park Boat Rentals is on Barton Creek, just north of Barton Springs. On the north side of the lake, Texas Rowing Center is at 1541 W. Cesar Chavez St.

9TH STREET BMX HILLS AND AUSTIN BMX SKATE PARK

If you like a bumpy bike ride, then you'll love the 9th Street BMX Hills in Duncan Park. You don't have to be an expert, because there's an area where beginners can learn to bunny hop and get used to sliding around on the dirt. It's also fun to watch the more experienced bikers on the really big jumps! Just a few blocks over, the Heath Eiland and Morgan Moss BMX Skate Park is a fun place to skate or bike in a bowl, on some ramps and through a street course.

FUN FACTS

» More than 25 years ago, a group of riders called the Ninth Street Locals sculpted the BMX hills with shovels.

» The hills are close to Shoal Creek, which overflows its banks every now and then, and floods the park. When that happens, the hardworking Ninth Street Locals come in and patch things up again.

» Named for two young men who loved biking and skating, the BMX Skate Park only exists because of Shoal Creek. It's built on a spot where a recreation center used to stand, but that building flooded every time the creek overflowed, and the city tore it down. Luckily, Austin leaders decided a skate park was the perfect thing to put in a flood plain.

THE LOWDOWN

» GEAR   Bike and skateboard, helmet, lots of water, courage.

» TELL YOUR PARENTS   Go early in the day, because the afternoon brings out more older kids and adults. If you are hungry after all that rolling around, there are lots of fun, casual restaurants you can walk to in this area, like Fresa's, Austin Java Company and Shoal Creek Saloon.

» KNOW BEFORE YOU GO   The hills are located at 900 W. 9th St., and the BMX Skate Park is at 1213 Shoal Creek Blvd. All the fun is free.

PADDLE & RIDE MISSION #3   AT 9TH STREET, FIND A MARKER THAT SAYS "SHOAL
CREEK TRAIL." FOLLOW THE PATH DOWN AND TAKE A LOOK AT THE CREEK.
IMAGINE WHAT KIND OF RAINSTORM WOULD CAUSE IT TO WASH OUT THE BMX HILLS!
(BONUS: IF YOU SEE ANY TRASH ON THE PATH, BE A FRIEND TO THE ENVIRONMENT AND THROW IT AWAY.
AUSTIN THANKS YOU VERY MUCH!)

GOOF OFF

WHEN FEELING BORED AND LAZY
CHECK OUT A LABYRINTH, BLACK LIGHTS OR HUGE T. REX.
BRING A FRIEND, ACT A LITTLE CRAZY.
SO MUCH TO DO, HERE IN AUSTIN T-X.

GLOW BOWLING AT THE UNION UNDERGROUND

Picture yourself walking through a huge college campus into a super-serious looking building filled with conference rooms, grownups and fancy staircases. Going into the basement of this building sounds dull and creepy, right? Sometimes, though, things aren't what they seem. Because this particular basement is called the Union Underground, and it is stocked with a bowling alley, air hockey and pool tables, and snacks. While that's all pretty cool, the capper is that the bowling alley is also filled with black light, which means you will glow when you bowl. That's right: YOU will glow. At least, your teeth and all other white stuff on your clothing will, which is the opposite of dull and just the right amount of creepy.

Design your own team bowling shirt. Come up with a name, team colors and logo.

 ## FUN FACTS

» You may have heard of ROY G BIV, an acronym for all the visible colors on the light spectrum (Red, orange, yellow, green, blue, indigo and violet). Well, black lights emit invisible ultra-violet rays, which make things called phosphors glow. It's the phosphors on your teeth, skin and clothing you see glowing under a black light.

» In bowling speak, three strikes in a row is called a turkey.

» The largest bowling alley in the world is in Japan. It has 116 lanes!

THE LOWDOWN

» **GEAR**   Socks, clothing with white for maximum glowability.

» **TELL YOUR PARENTS**   Parking is available in several nearby lots, including one at 2214 San Antonio St. for $3/hour. Each player can choose whether they want regular or bumper bowling.

» **KNOW BEFORE YOU GO**   Glow bowling is located in the Texas Union Underground. The official address is 2308 Whitis, but you can enter through doors that face the West Mall on the UT campus (the first building off Guadalupe St. directly west of the UT Tower). Games cost $3 per person and shoe rental is $2 per pair. Check universityunions.utexas.edu for additional information. (512-475-6670)

GOOF OFF MISSION #1   WACKY BOWL ON AT LEAST THREE FRAMES OF YOUR GAME. FOR EXAMPLE: 1) BOWL DOING YOUR BEST IMPRESSION OF A SLOTH, 2) BOWL BACKWARDS, 3) BOWL WHILE SINGING, "GOODNESS GRACIOUS, GREAT BOWLING BALLS OF FIRE!"

GOOF OFF MISSION #2   PICK YOUR FAVORITE SCULPTURE AND GET YOUR PICTURE TAKEN WITH IT. ALSO, YELL "FORE!" BEFORE YOUR FIRST PUTT ON THE 12TH HOLE, THEN WAVE AT ALL OF THE OTHER MINI GOLFERS WHEN THEY GIVE YOU A FUNNY LOOK.

PETER PAN MINI GOLF

You may have played miniature golf, but you've never played it anywhere like Peter Pan Mini Golf…unless you've hit a golf ball through a towering T. Rex, high-top sneaker, whale's mouth or well-dressed pig. There are two 18-hole courses to choose from, and beginners will have as much fun as experts.

FUN FACTS

» Peter Pan Mini Golf opened more than 60 years ago, in 1948. In 2011, the cement sculptures were starting to crumble, so a local artist gave them a facelift.

» Before the makeover, the Converse sneaker sculpture was painted to look like the "old woman who lived in a shoe" nursery rhyme.

THE LOWDOWN

» GEAR   Comfy clothes and shoes, your very best golf swing.

» TELL YOUR PARENTS   You'll need cash or a check, and you can BYOB as long as there is no glass in your cooler.

» KNOW BEFORE YOU GO   Peter Pan is located at 1207 Barton Springs Rd., just down the road from Butler Park. Big kids cost $6 for 18 holes and $9 for 36, and you can play from mid-morning until at least 10PM almost every day of the week. Check peterpanminigolf.com for additional info. (512-472-1033)

BUTLER PARK

Tired of the same old monkey bars? Then Butler Park is for you! There's a spiral path that magically appears when you climb Doug Sahm Hill, a huge map of Texas to run around on, the awesome Liz Carpenter spray pad that lights up at night, a cool stone labyrinth to wander in, a wide open grassy field for soccer or a picnic and a long and winding paved sidewalk that's perfect for biking, scooting or skating. With so many fun activities, the only problem is deciding which part of the park to explore first (and maybe convincing your parents to stay just a little bit longer).

FUN FACTS

» Doug Sahm was a super-talented musician famous for lots of things, like writing a song called "Beautiful Texas Sunshine" and being in a Tejano band called the "Texas Tornados." Tejano (or Tex-Mex) is a kind of music that was born in Texas but can also sound a little like polka, pop, Latin and R&B.

» Liz Carpenter was a funny journalist and feminist who lived from 1920 to 2010. She was the first female student body vice president at Austin High School.

» The path labyrinth near Barton Springs Rd. is called a "Chartres" labyrinth since it looks like one in a famous French cathedral. Make your way into the center "heart space." Clap your hands and listen to the squeaky echo.

THE LOWDOWN

» GEAR Bike, scooter or roller skates; helmet, picnic, water, swimsuit, towel, sunscreen and water shoes.

» TELL YOUR PARENTS If you need a cool treat after you play, the legendary Sandy's Frozen Custard shop is a short walk east on Barton Springs Rd.

» KNOW BEFORE YOU GO Butler Park is located at 1000 Barton Springs Rd. There are several free, small parking lots nearby—one at the Dougherty Arts Center on Barton Springs, and a few on Riverside Drive. You can also pay to park in the Long Center lot next door.

GOOF OFF MISSION #3   RUN, ROLL OR SCOOT UP DOUG SAHM HILL, FIND
AUSTIN ON THE TEXAS MAP AND HOP FIVE TIMES ON ONE FOOT. BE BOLD ON
YOUR WAY DOWN THE HILL, AND YELL AT THE TOP OF YOUR LUNGS, "BEAUTIFUL
TEXAS SUNSHINE."

35

ROAD TRIP

WHERE SHOULD WE GO ON A SHORT JOY RIDE?
MAYBE CLIMB A GRANITE DOME.
ROPE SWINGS, WATER SLIDES,
SO MUCH FUN, AWAY FROM HOME.

Don't Mess
With Texas
UP TO $2000 FINE
FOR LITTERING

BLUE HOLE REGIONAL PARK

Of all the great places in Texas to swim, Blue Hole on Cypress Creek may be the very best. It's oh-so pretty, and there are not one, but TWO awesome cypress tree swings that can launch you right into the water. There's also a shallow end to wade into if you are a professional rock hunter, and an area for floating on a tube. When your fingers begin to prune, go lounge on the grassy picnic area and let the sun warm you up, or check out miles of hiking trails.

FUN FACTS

» Some of the bald cypress trees at Blue Hole are 200-300 years old. They are called "bald" because they drop their leaves in the winter.

» The water at Blue Hole is so clear, in part, because Cypress Creek is fed by a natural spring. Also, rainwater that flows into the creek is filtered through "Texas holey rock," which is limestone that looks like Swiss cheese thanks to prehistoric organisms making holes in it.

THE LOWDOWN

» **GEAR**   Swimsuit, towel, picnic, lounge chairs, small float, water shoes.

» **TELL YOUR PARENTS**   Get there early! Blue Hole is very popular in summer, and the doors may close temporarily when it fills up with visitors. If you want to make a day of it, Wimberley has many cute shops and restaurants, and a wonderful children's theater called the EmilyAnn. On the drive back to Austin, Pieous in Dripping Springs is a delicious pizza stop.

» **KNOW BEFORE YOU GO**   Blue Hole Regional Park is located at 100 Blue Hole Ln. in Wimberley, about 45 minutes from Austin. The park is free, but the swimming area costs $9 for adults and $5 for kids 4-12. It's a nice place to explore any time of year, but you can only swim in summer months from 10AM to dusk. (512-660-9111)

ROAD TRIP MISSION #1   PICK A SWING, HOLD ON AS LONG AS YOU CAN AND YODEL YOUR VERY BEST TARZAN VICTORY YELL BEFORE SPLASHING DOWN INTO THE WATER.

ROAD TRIP MISSION #2   ON THE WEST SIDE OF THE PARK, CHALLENGE A FRIEND TO COMPETE ON THE DOWNHILL RACER. ON THE EAST SIDE, DO THE SAME ON THE BLACK KNIGHT. THE SLIPPERIEST SLIDER PICKS THE NEXT RIDE.

SCHLITTERBAHN WATER PARK

Pretty much any adventure that requires an inner tube and a bathing suit is going to be awesome, right? Well, of all the places that require both of those things, Schlitterbahn Water Park is probably the coolest. That's because it has so many water slides, raft rides, wet playgrounds, wave pools, twisty tubes and wild rapids that you can't possibly do them all in a single day. If you talk your parents into going, keep in mind these two things: you will have one of the most thrilling theme park experiences of your entire life, and you will be exhausted and waterlogged at the end of the day.

 FUN FACTS

» Schlitterbahn opened in 1979 in New Braunfels, a town established in 1845 by a German prince. The water park owners were thinking of that European heritage when they made up a name that combined the German words for slippery (schlitter) and road (bahn).

» The west side of the park uses spring-fed water from the Comal River for lots of fun rides. The Comal is very short, and one of only two rivers where the endangered fountain darter fish makes its home.

THE LOWDOWN

» **GEAR** Swimsuit, water shoes, towel, sunscreen, cooler full of lunch, snacks and drinks.

» **TELL YOUR PARENTS** Tickets can be a bit cheaper if you purchase in advance online, or from a Kroger or HEB store. The park is divided into the older west side and newer east side, and provides a free shuttle bus to take you in between.

» **KNOW BEFORE YOU GO** Schlitterbahn is located at 400 N. Liberty Ave. in New Braunfels, about 45 minutes from Austin. Plan to get there a bit before it opens, and park near the section where you want to leave your cooler. If bought online, full-price tickets in summer 2016 were about $51 for adults and $39 for kids. Check schlitterbahn.com for current info. (1-830-625-2351)

ENCHANTED ROCK STATE NATURAL AREA

Everything is bigger in Texas—even the rocks! The ginormous salmon-colored Enchanted Rock, for example, is so big that you can see it from miles and miles away. This beautiful hunk of granite is a very special geological feature called a batholith, and it's a whopping 425 feet taller than anything around it…which means it absolutely, positively has to be climbed. It also begs to be circled, stood atop, wandered into and generally explored. There is lots of nature to watch out for, like lizards, vultures and prickly pear shrubs. On top of the dome, water collects in low spots, forming super special vernal pools, which are home to tiny little fairy shrimp—one of the most important links in the E-Rock food chain!

"X" marks the spot of E-Rock's dark skies. Color in this light pollution map. Note how red Austin and San Antonio are. They both rate 7 or higher on the Bortle Scale.

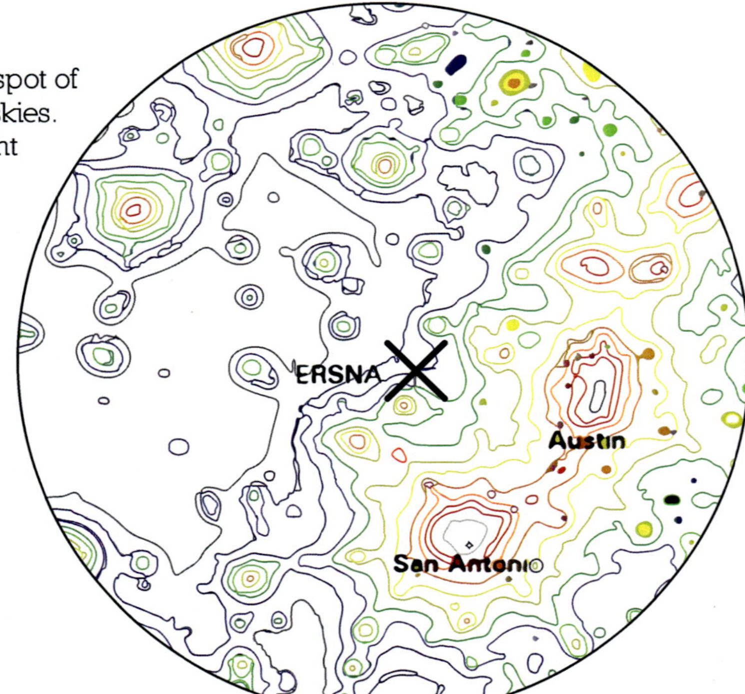

 FUN FACTS

» The E-Rock batholith started forming a billion years ago, when it was part of a huge pool of hot magma. It pushed up, cooled, and, after a very long time, turned into the pink granite dome you see today. Even though the part you can climb is huge, most of the batholith's 62 square miles are underground!

» Enchanted Rock is a recognized "Dark Sky Place," which means every effort is made to ensure the area is dark enough for visitors to see the big and bright Texas stars. Darkness is measured from 1 to 9 on the "Bortle Scale," and E-Rock is rated 3.

» Humans camped here around 12,000 years ago, and there are more than 400 archaeological sites in the park.

 THE LOWDOWN

» GEAR Walking shoes, lots of water, sunscreen and snacks.

» TELL YOUR PARENTS Nearby Fredericksburg is a cute place to get lunch and check out the National Museum of the Pacific War. E-Rock is a great place to camp, but you'll need to reserve early at tpwd.texas.gov.

» KNOW BEFORE YOU GO Enchanted Rock is located at 16710 Ranch Rd. 965 near Fredericksburg, a beautiful 90-minute drive from Austin. It fills up on holidays and weekends, so plan to get there early in the day. $7 for adults; kids 12 and under are free. (830-685-3636)

ROAD TRIP MISSION #3   CLIMB ALL THE WAY TO THE TOP OF ENCHANTED ROCK, OF COURSE, AND SEE IF YOU CAN FIND A DELICATE VERNAL POOL ON THE DOME. ON THE WAY UP, TELL YOUR PARENTS YOU KNOW THEY CAN DO IT!

BIG TOP
SHO... SODA

SHOP

SO MANY THINGS ON YOUR MUST-HAVE LIST:
GUMMIES, CAPS, BOOKS AND SOUVENIR TEES,
WIND-UP TOYS, BANDS FOR YOUR WRIST.
YOUR FOLKS MAY SAY "YES" IF YOU SAY "PLEASE."

BOOKPEOPLE

Calling all bookworms! Every vacation should include some time spent with a page-turner, and BookPeople is the perfect place to find a stellar story to read while you're hanging out at the park, lounging at a swimming hole or riding in the car. They've got gobs of graphic novels, a plethora of picture books, beaucoup biographies and scads of series. Grab a parent by the hand, take them upstairs and pick something magical, nutty, sad or spooky. If you aren't sure what you're in the mood for, ask one of the friendly folks in the Book Kids section for an always-awesome suggestion.

 FUN FACTS

» BookPeople opened in 1970 and is the LARGEST independent bookstore in Texas. There are around 400,000 books on the shelves!

» Independent bookstores are not part of a corporate chain, and the only BookPeople on the whole planet is right here in Austin. Lucky us!

» Texas has its very own prize for children's literature called the Bluebonnet Award, and the store has a special section for Bluebonnet books, as well as Newbery and Caldecott winners.

 THE LOWDOWN

» TELL YOUR PARENTS   The store is near the 9th Street BMX Hills as well as Pease Park, a great place to bike and play on Kingsbury St.

» KNOW BEFORE YOU GO   Open from 9AM to 11PM, BookPeople is located at 603 N. Lamar Blvd. The bookstore has a coffee shop with snacks, and plenty of parking in the adjacent lot. Go to bookpeople.com for information about the store's many kid events. (512-472-5050)

Fill in these book spines with titles of books you love.

SHOP MISSION #1   ASK FOR A COMMUNITY BOOK REVIEW CARD AT THE INFORMATION DESK JUST INSIDE THE STORE ENTRANCE, AND WRITE A REVIEW OF YOUR FAVORITE BOOK (EXTRA POINTS FOR CHOOSING THIS BOOK)!

TOY JOY

With a name like "Toy Joy," you know this store is going to be awesome. The secret is to go in with an open mind, rather than to look for something specific. If you do, you are sure to find something wacky and amazing. It is easy to talk parents into taking you to Toy Joy because it is the kind of place grownups like almost as much as kids. Pro Tip: Ask a parent if they had a favorite character from Hello Kitty or Smurfs or Teenage Mutant Ninja Turtles. Listen to them tell their story, give them a hug, then say you want to take THEM to Toy Joy to pick out something special.

FUN FACTS

» If you wander up or down 2nd Street, you'll cross streets named for Texas rivers going in the same order they run through the state. At each intersection, you'll find art that represents that river. The closest one to Toy Joy is Guadalupe St.

» Your four-footed siblings are welcome in Toy Joy, so feel free to bring Fido into the store!

THE LOWDOWN

» **TELL YOUR PARENTS** Toy Joy is part of the 2nd Street Shopping District, and there are lots of great places to eat and shop within walking distance. Also, there's a terrific farmer's market a few blocks away at 422 Guadalupe St. on Saturdays from 9AM to 1PM.

» **KNOW BEFORE YOU GO** Toy Joy is located at 403 W. 2nd St. and is open from (at least) 10AM to 8PM every day of the week. The store offers two hours of free validated parking in the nearby City Hall or AMLI garages. Visit toyjoy.com for more info. (512-320-0090)

SOCO: BIG TOP CANDY SHOP

South Congress Avenue (AKA SoCo) is one of the coolest streets in Austin. If you drive downhill and catch the stoplights just right, it's like a roller coaster ride with an amazing view of the State Capitol. It also runs right over the bat bridge (see page 22) and has unique stores for everyone in the family. The very best one for kids, though, is Big Top Candy Shop. Pretty much all you need to know about Big Top is that it's home to more than 300 kinds of serve-yourself candy and 2,000 kinds of wrapped candy, including: chocolate rocks, gummy sharks, taffy, licorice whips, exploding cinnamon candy, Tart 'n Tinys, ring pops, all-day suckers, bubble gum that looks like crayons, marshmallow fluff, jelly beans, Circus Peanuts and Pop Rocks. You might also need to know they have ice cream, shaved ice and an old-fashioned soda fountain. Other than that, you don't need to know anything else.

FUN FACTS

» Congress Avenue was designed in the 1830s but didn't go south of the river until the city built a bridge in 1910. Traffic included horse-drawn buggies, electric streetcars and the occasional cow.

» There are some really cool painted murals on SoCo, including one on Jo's Coffee Shop that says "I Love You So Much" and another on the side of SoCo Books that illustrates "The New Austin."

THE LOWDOWN

» **TELL YOUR PARENTS** There are lots of great places to shop and eat within walking distance of Big Top. Home Slice Pizza, Torchy's Tacos and Hopdoddy burgers are favorite restaurants. Further down Congress, Uncommon Objects has lots of weird and wonderful things to check out, and Parts & Labour has fun T-shirts. SoCo gets packed on the weekend, so it's best to go early. Since parking can be tricky, you may have to walk a few blocks. Luckily, every block is packed with fun things to see.

» **KNOW BEFORE YOU GO** The store is located at 1706 South Congress Ave., and is open every day at least from 11AM to 7PM. (512-462-2220)

👍 SHOP MISSION #3   FIND "THE NEW AUSTIN" MURAL A FEW BLOCKS DOWN FROM BIG TOP.
POINT TO THE ROCKET POP, CUPCAKE TRAILER AND BATS. TELL YOUR PARENTS WHY YOU
THINK SOME OF THE MURAL IS LEFT UNFINISHED.

EXPLORE

THE WILD IS CALLING YOUR ADVENTUROUS HEART TO CREEKS, ROCK ISLANDS AND WOODSY FRONTIERS. AMELIA EARHART, LEWIS & CLARK MAKE YOUR OWN PATH, BRAVE PIONEER.

BARTON CREEK GREENBELT

Austin is a big city, but it's also a wild and rocky wilderness when you're adventuring along the 7.8 miles of Barton Creek that run right through the middle of town. Depending on the weather and where you enter the Greenbelt trail, there are great spots for hopping rocks on mountain bikes, scaling limestone walls and swinging into the creek. Or, you can just hike around, find some boulders to scramble over and search for heart-shaped rocks. You might even spot a cave, or uncover a hidden geocache (...unless you're a Muggle*).

*hint: Geocaching.com

FUN FACTS

» In total, Barton Creek flows along for 40 miles until it reaches its mouth on the Colorado River right at Lady Bird Lake.

» There are all kinds of pretty plants to spot around here, including dogwoods, redbuds, junipers, red cardinal flowers, and pretty yellow Maximilian sunflowers.

THE LOWDOWN

» GEAR   Sturdy shoes that can get wet, plenty of water, sunscreen, snacks.

» TELL YOUR PARENTS   There are lots of entrances to the Greenbelt, so pick yours based on what you want to do. The trailhead is flat, and convenient if you're at Barton Springs. Campbell's Hole has neighborhood parking and a short, rocky hike to the creek. Gus Fruh also has neighborhood parking and a nice swimming hole if the creek is full. The main entrance has an office parking lot with access to a rockier terrain. The Hill of Life has neighborhood parking and is a good access point via a very steep hill to beautiful Sculpture Falls.

» KNOW BEFORE YOU GO
Trailhead: 2201 Barton Springs Rd.; Campbell's Hole: 2010 Home Dale Dr.; Gus Fruh: 2642 Barton Hills Dr.; Main Entrance: 3755-B Capital of Texas Highway; Hill of Life: 1710 Camp Craft Rd.

EXPLORE MISSION #1 IF YOU DON'T ALREADY KNOW, FIND OUT WHAT GEOCACHING IS, AND LOCATE THE CACHE NEAREST YOUR ENTRANCE ON THE GREENBELT. BE SURE AND BRING SOMETHING TO LEAVE BEHIND IF YOU WANT TO TAKE SOMETHING WITH YOU.

EXPLORE MISSION #2   FIND THE MOONTOWER ON THE SOUTH SIDE OF BARTON SPRINGS ROAD. LAY ON THE GROUND UNDER IT, AND SAY THIS LINE FROM THE SHEL SILVERSTEIN POEM, "MOON-CATCHIN' NET": I'VE MADE ME A MOON-CATCHIN' NET,/ AND I'M GOIN' HUNTIN' TONIGHT,/I'LL RUN ALONG SWINGIN' IT OVER MY HEAD,/AND GRAB FOR THAT BIG BALL OF LIGHT.

ZILKER PARK

Zilker Park is really a collection of many different parks, which means there's lots to choose from and something for everyone! If you're looking for a place to play soccer, fly a kite, climb on a rock island or just hang out on a comfy blanket with a popsicle, the Great Lawn is where it's at. If you're in the mood for activities, though, you can play disc golf or sand volleyball, and the beautiful Botanical Garden has a fairy house trail and pioneer village. The Austin Nature and Science Center is way more fun that it sounds because you can see rescued critters like owls and wildcats, hunt for fossil casts in a dino pit, watch bees at work in a bustling hive, and swap feathers, rocks and other found objects for treasures at a trade counter.

 FUN FACTS

» The 351-acre park is named for Andrew Jackson Zilker, a man who made a fortune selling ice, and who donated land that would eventually become Austin's most famous park.

» Zilker Park is home to one of Austin's many special moontowers. Brought to the city in 1894, the 165-foot tall towers illuminated a 1,500-foot-radius circle. Austin may be the only place in the world that still has moontowers!

 THE LOWDOWN

» GEAR Sturdy shoes, soccer ball or frisbee, picnic blanket, water, snacks.

» TELL YOUR PARENTS Zilker Park consists of other fun places mentioned in this book, like Barton Springs Pool (and the Zilker Zephyr) and Umlauf Sculpture Garden. There is street parking (fee on weekends March-Sept.) for the Great Lawn on Lou Neff Rd., and field lot parking on Stratford Dr. Go early if you can!

» KNOW BEFORE YOU GO Zilker Botanical Garden is located at 2200 Barton Springs Rd. and is open from 9AM to 5PM almost every day. Entry ranges from $1 to $3 (cash or check) (512-477-8672). Austin Nature and Science Center is located at 2389 Stratford Dr. and is open from 9AM to 5PM Monday through Saturday and noon to 5PM on Sundays. Free entry. (512-974-3888)

LADY BIRD JOHNSON WILDFLOWER CENTER

Don't be fooled by the word "flower." This place is way more than a garden. It's kind of magical, like stepping through the wardrobe into Narnia after the White Witch is defeated. Flowers are blooming, creatures are stirring and everyone is peaceful, playful and happy. As you walk under the aqueduct, imagine you're entering your own secret kingdom where you can quietly track creatures like roadrunners and deer, or peep into a wetland pond and spy the most humongous tadpole you've ever seen. Wander through the inspirational gardens and decide which one you want behind your castle. Then, go to the Family Garden, where anything is possible.

As you wander around the Wildflower Center, fill in this flowerbed with drawings of the plants and flowers you like most. Make sure you label them, so you remember your favorites.

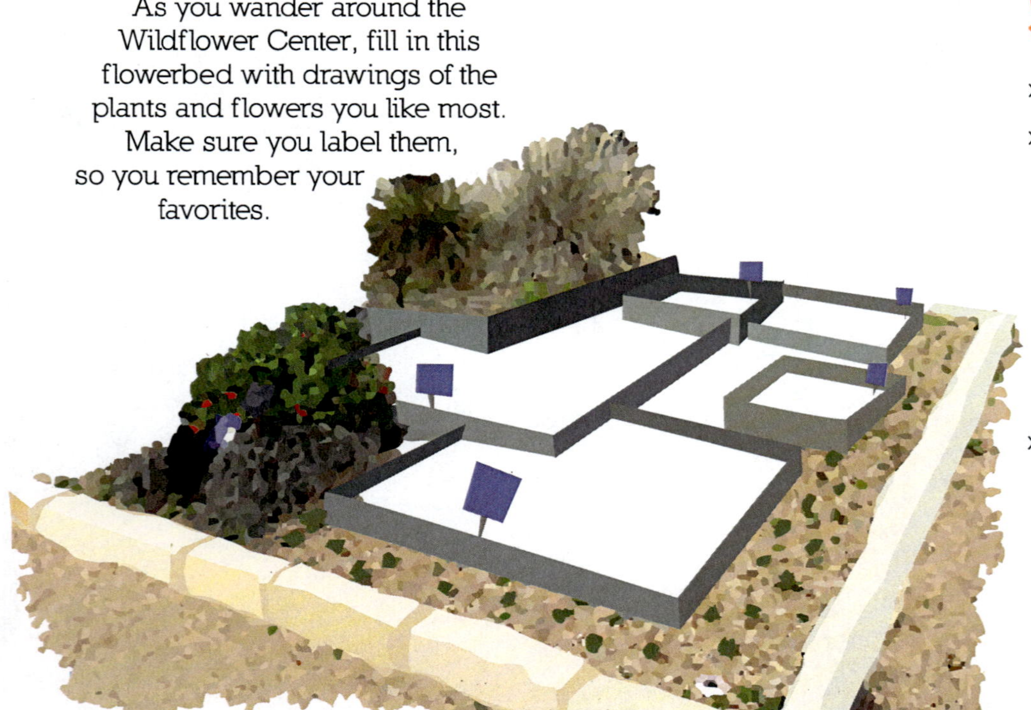

FUN FACTS

» Lady Bird Johnson was a very smart person and environmentalist. She was married to President Lyndon B. Johnson, and worked hard her whole life to make sure that nature is important to all Americans. Her childhood nurse, Alice Tittle, once said she was as "pretty as a ladybird," and the nickname stuck!

» An aqueduct is a manmade channel for carrying water, often in the form of a bridge with columns. The one here helps collect 70,000 gallons of rainwater used around the center.

» In a tight race against the cotton boll and cactus flower, the bluebonnet was voted in as the Texas state flower in 1901.

THE LOWDOWN

» **GEAR**   Comfy clothes and shoes, water.

» **TELL YOUR PARENTS**   Be sure and check out a discovery pack from the admission kiosk. There is a little café on the grounds where you can get a snack, and the nearby Veloway (you'll drive right by it on the way) is a paved three-mile track to skate or bike on if you bring some wheels.

» **KNOW BEFORE YOU GO**   Located at 4801 La Crosse Ave., the Wildflower Center is open from 9AM to 5PM in spring. To find out hours in other times of the year, visit wildflower.org. Entry is $10 for adults and $4 for kids. (512-232-0100)

EXPLORE MISSION #3   COMPLETE THIS OBSTACLE COURSE THROUGH THE
FAMILY GARDEN: 1) DO YOUR VERY BEST BIRD IMPRESSION IN A GIANT NEST,
2) JUMP ACROSS THREE STUMPS OR LOGS WITHOUT TOUCHING THE GROUND,
3) HOP ON ONE FOOT ACROSS THE HOPSCOTCH PATH, 4) GO BEHIND THE WATERFALL
AND MAKE UP A SHORT STORY ABOUT ONE OF THE PICTOGRAPHS, 5) FIND YOUR WAY
THROUGH THE METAMORPHOSIS MAZE.

ZOLTAR

BIG NIGHT OUT

WHAT'S THAT? YOU SAY YOU'RE BORED?
WELL, PICK A FUN PLACE AND GRAB MOM AND DAD.

MOVIES, MUSIC, GAMES GALORE,
FAMILY NIGHT IS SUPER RAD!

ALAMO DRAFTHOUSE

There are movie theaters and then there are MOVIE THEATERS. The Alamo Drafthouse is definitely the second kind. For one thing, it's more of a small movie *stadium* than a movie theater, so you'll always be able to see around the big-haired lady seated in front of you. You also get to order your popcorn, milkshake, burger, pizza, pretzel or soba noodle salad (hey—it could happen, right?) inside the theater and eat it from your own little table right in front of you. Best of all, the Alamo plays all the new movies AND some awesome old ones you might never get to see on the big screen otherwise. Imagine a 20-foot-tall Totoro or Iron Giant, and you'll get the picture.

FUN FACTS

» While the Alamo Drafthouse now has a chain of theaters in cities across America, it started right here in Austin in 1997.

» The very first public movie theater in the United States opened in Pittsburgh in 1905. It was called "The Nickelodeon," and the first movie they showed was *The Great Train Robbery*.

THE LOWDOWN

» **TELL YOUR PARENTS**   In the summertime, Alamo theaters offer cheap movies during their Kids Camp.

» **KNOW BEFORE YOU GO**   There are several Alamo Drafthouse locations scattered around town, and all of them have online reserved seating. Check alamodrafthouse.com for special events, to see what's playing near you, and to reserve your spot ahead of time!

Now Showing! Pretend your Austin adventure is a movie, and make a title and poster for it in this frame.

BIG NIGHT OUT MISSION #1   THE ALAMO HAS MOVIE POSTERS ALL OVER THE LOBBY AND HALLS. FIND ONE THAT INTRIGUES YOU AND FIND OUT WHAT YEAR THE MOVIE WAS MADE, WHO DIRECTED IT, WHO STARRED IN IT AND WHY IT IS FAMOUS.

BIG NIGHT OUT MISSION #2   BORROW A GROWNUP'S PHONE, AND DO A LETTER SCAVENGER HUNT. THERE ARE LOTS OF SIGNS AROUND ABGB, SO TAKE PICTURES OF LETTERS THAT SPELL OUT YOUR NAME. SHOW THESE COOL PICS TO YOUR PARENTS.

THE ABGB

You know how parents like to go to restaurants and sit around and talk? You know how you are DONE with that situation after about 30 minutes? Well, the Austin Beer Garden Brewing Company (ABGB) is the kind of place where parents get to sit around and talk while you pretend you live in a tree fort. If you grab a table down in the shade, you can be near your folks while basically forgetting you're in a restaurant at all. Then the pizza or sandwich you wanted will arrive at the long wooden picnic table where the adults have been happily chatting while you were happily petting pups, playing cards, or making a new friend who brought a super-cool yo-yo. That's called a win-win.

FUN FACTS

» People have been brewing and drinking beer in some form since 3000 BC or earlier!

» Most beer is made from a few basic ingredients: barley, hops, yeast and water.

THE LOWDOWN.

» TELL YOUR PARENTS   The ABGB often has midday music on weekends. You'll find lots of families enjoying good eats all day.

» KNOW BEFORE YOU GO   The ABGB is located at 1305 W. Oltorf. It is closed on Monday but opens by noon all other days. Check theabgb.com for music listings and special events. (512-298-2242)

PINBALLZ ARCADE

Before there was Minecraft or even Pac-Man, there was pinball. Even fancily dressed French people played a version of it way back in the 1700s! An activity that's lasted that long is bound to be worth doing—especially when it's in a place with hundreds of other fun games to choose from. Remember the movie *Wreck-It Ralph*? Well, Pinballz is a lot like the arcade where the Sugar Rush and Fix-It Felix games live…only much, much bigger. There are hundreds of pinball machines, vintage video games like Tron and Frogger, skee-ball, fortune-telling machines and other games. Oh, and there are lots of games that crank out cute strips of red tickets to trade in for all kinds of fun prizes. Good luck!

FUN FACTS

» The first coin-operated pinball machine was developed in the 1930s. Oftentimes, you'd get five to seven balls for one penny.

THE LOWDOWN

» **TELL YOUR PARENTS** Most of the machines are token operated, so bring dollars to trade in. There are lots of kid-friendly places near Pinballz to round out a fun evening, including an Alamo Drafthouse location (2700 W. Anderson Ln.), Terra Toys (2438 W. Anderson Ln.), P. Terry's (drive-thru only at 8515 Burnet Rd.), Lucy's Fried Chicken (5408 Burnet Rd.) and the very nice Beverly S. Sheffield neighborhood park (7000 Ardath St.).

» **KNOW BEFORE YOU GO** Pinballz is located 15 to 20 minutes north of downtown at 8940 Research Blvd. Kids are welcome from 10AM until 10PM every day. (512-420-8458)

BIG NIGHT OUT MISSION #3   CHALLENGE YOUR PARENT TO A SKEE-BALL CONTEST. ASK NICELY IF THEY'LL DONATE THEIR RED TICKETS TO YOU.

WONDER

PICTURE *YOUR* ART ON A BIG MUSEUM WALL.
IT TOOK MANY LONG HOURS TO MAKE IT JUST SO!
SCULPTURES OF JUNK, MAGNIFICENT SCRAWLS,
YOU MIGHT BE THE NEXT PICASSO, YOU KNOW.

THE CONTEMPORARY AUSTIN — LAGUNA GLORIA

If your idea of a great museum is one where you can spin 'round and 'round, laugh, and talk as loud as you want about what you are seeing, you will love Laguna Gloria. That's because all of the art is outside, scattered around tall trees, grassy fields, fancy gardens, and the shores of a shimmering lake. It's the perfect place for a scavenger hunt and to talk about why each larger-than-life artwork (like Miffy) is special enough to live in this gorgeous habitat.

FUN FACTS

» Laguna Gloria means "heavenly lagoon."

» The beautiful villa was built in 1916 by a woman named Clara Driscoll. She was a philanthropist and historic preservationist, which means she donated her own money to save buildings. She donated Laguna Gloria so the people of Austin would have a beautiful museum.

» "Miffy" is the English name of a Dutch picture book character created by Dick Bruna. In the Netherlands, they call her "Nijntje" (pronounced "nine-cha"), which means "little rabbit."

THE LOWDOWN

» **GEAR**   Comfy shoes, water.

» **TELL YOUR PARENTS**   Pick up an action pack at the villa's reception desk. Also, check the event calendar on thecontemporaryaustin.org if you want to pop in during one of their many family events. If you have time and energy before or after your visit, add on a free walk next door to see some beautiful peacocks at Mayfield Park, or drive to nearby Mt. Bonnell and hike up the steps for a lovely view over Austin.

» **KNOW BEFORE YOU GO**   Located at 3809 W. 35th St., Laguna Gloria is open Monday through Saturday from 9AM to 5PM and Sundays from 10AM to 5PM. Adults cost $5 and kids under 18 get in for free. (512-458-8191)

WONDER MISSION #1   GRAB AN ACTION PACK FROM THE RECEPTION DESK AND
DESIGN YOUR OWN FIVE-SCULPTURE SCAVENGER HUNT. WHEN YOU FIND "LOOKING
UP," ACTUALLY LOOK UP AND DO YOUR VERY FASTEST ARMS-OUTSTRETCHED SPIN
FIVE TIMES. THEN FALL DOWN.

WONDER MISSION #2 FIND "LOTUS" AND TAKE A VOTE ON WHETHER HE'S THE CUTEST ANIMAL IN THE SCULPTURE GARDEN.

72

UMLAUF SCULPTURE GARDEN

Have you ever created 100 of anything? Like, have you ever scored 100 soccer goals, made 100 loom bracelets, drawn 100 pictures of Totoro, or maybe played "Oh! Susanna" 100 times on the harmonica? If you have, well, you deserve a super special reward! Most people (grownups included) haven't, though, which is one of the many reasons the Umlauf Sculpture Garden is something pretty magical. Every single artwork you'll see in this peaceful place was created by one man—Charles Umlauf (rhymes with zoom-cowf). Even though the sculptures are very different, he created the beautiful big-handed mamas with babies, the falling winged Icarus, the powerful ice skater your parent will ask you to mimic, and even the menagerie of animals you'll want to take home and put in your own garden.

FUN FACTS

» Charles Umlauf's sculptures are in museums all over the United States, including the Smithsonian Institution in Washington, DC, and the Metropolitan Museum of Art in New York City.

» In Greek mythology, Icarus was a young man whose dad made him wings of feathers and wax, warning that he should not fly too close to the sun. Icarus didn't listen, and his wings melted. You can read a bit about Icarus in the Percy Jackson books.

THE LOWDOWN

» GEAR   Comfy shoes, water, hands ready to touch the bronze statues (but not the stone ones).

» TELL YOUR PARENTS   Umlauf is a small place, and a great activity to combine with Barton Springs, which has an entrance right across the street. Also, the museum holds lots of fun, kid-friendly activities during the week, as well as special camps and activities during the summer.

» KNOW BEFORE YOU GO   Umlauf Sculpture Garden is located at 605 Robert E. Lee Rd. It's open from 10AM to 4PM Tuesday through Friday and noon to 4PM on Saturday and Sunday. Adult entry is $5, students are $1 and children 12 and under are free. See what's happening in the garden at umlaufsculpture.org. (512-445-5582)

CATHEDRAL OF JUNK

Have you ever heard the saying, "One man's trash is another man's treasure"? If you get to visit the Cathedral of Junk, you will give that idea a lot of thought. First, though, you will have the craziest game of hide-and-seek or make believe you've ever had. Why? This is not a building FULL of junk, but a giant playhouse MADE of things like broken statues, tires, computers, dolls, mirrors, telephones, records and…almost anything and everything someone would normally throw out. It is beautiful in a weird way, and so full of imagination that you will easily turn its many rooms, staircases, king-size chairs, and super-fast slide into your own little world. Will you be an orphan in a hideout, a prince in a castle, or maybe a stray dog in a junkyard? It all depends on your point of view.

Fill in this architectural rendering of the Cathedral of Junk. Feel free to add stuff of your own!

FUN FACTS

» Vince Hanneman started building the Cathedral of Junk in 1989 and continues to add on when he feels inspired.

» The world's best playhouse is made of more than 60 TONS of junk. That's 120,000 pounds!

THE LOWDOWN

» GEAR   Sturdy shoes, water, and clothes made for climbing.

» TELL YOUR PARENTS   See if you can talk them into taking you for some ice cream after your adventure. Delicious Dolce Neve at 1713 S. 1st St. may be the closest, but Amy's Ice Cream at 2901 S. Lamar Blvd. has a good outdoor playground, as well as a burger joint called Phil's under the same roof.

» KNOW BEFORE YOU GO The Cathedral of Junk is located in a backyard at 4422 Lareina Dr., and you can only visit by calling to make an appointment with artist/homeowner Vince Hanneman. There is no bathroom here, and a $10 donation per group is recommended. (512-299-7413)

WONDER MISSION #3   LOOK INTO A MIRROR AND PRETEND YOU ARE LIKE ALICE
STEPPING THROUGH THE LOOKING GLASS INTO A COMPLETELY DIFFERENT WONDERLAND.
TELL YOUR FRIENDS OR PARENTS WHAT WORLD YOU'VE IMAGINED.

DISCOVER

PRESIDENTS, SPACE MISSIONS AND SETTLERS WHO GOT STRANDED. YEP, TEXAS HAS A PRETTY COOL PAST. REMEMBER THE ALAMO! THE EAGLE HAS LANDED! SOME HISTORY LESSONS ARE REALLY A BLAST.

DISCOVER MISSION #1   FIND THE MARBLE BUST OF MIRIAM AMANDA WALLACE "MA" FERGUSON, THE FIRST WOMAN GOVERNOR OF TEXAS, AND TELL HER, "HOWDY, MA!"

THE TEXAS CAPITOL

There are lots of good reasons to visit the Texas Capitol, including the fact that it's the BIGGEST state capitol in all of America. But it's way more than just a big, red building—it's a big, red building where elected lawmakers make important decisions that affect your life. If you take a tour of the Capitol, you can see the roomy rooms where Congress meets to make laws; wave hello at a life-size statue of the "Father of Texas," Stephen F. Austin; see a painting of Alamo hero David Crockett holding his coonskin cap and stand in the middle of a cavernous rotunda. Be sure and take a look at the six seals in the middle of the floor, which represent the countries that have ruled Texas. Clap your hands in the middle and listen to the echo.

Fill in these empty seals with the other five countries that have governed Texas.

FUN FACTS

» The Goddess of Liberty atop the Capitol is a much lighter aluminum copy of the 3,000-pound original that was there from 1888 to 1985. You can see her over at the Bullock History Museum. (Looking good, old lady!)

» The star in the Capitol dome is around 218 feet above the floor and measures eight feet across.

» The Capitol is made of Sunset Red granite rock from nearby Granite Mountain.

» The Six Flags amusement park chain started in Texas in 1961. The original park was divided into six sections named for each country that has governed Texas.

THE LOWDOWN

» GEAR   Comfy shoes and stamina for walking up and down some stairwells.

» TELL YOUR PARENTS   There are free basic tours throughout the day, but special tours are also available, so call for a schedule. On the southeast corner of the grounds, the Texas Capitol Visitors Center has cool exhibits, too! There is a nice cafeteria in the Capitol extension.

» KNOW BEFORE YOU GO   The Capitol is located at 1100 Congress Ave. It's open Monday through Friday from 7AM to 10PM and Saturday and Sunday from 9AM to 8PM. Parking is free for two hours in the parking garage at 1201 San Jacinto. (512-463-0063)

BULLOCK TEXAS STATE HISTORY MUSEUM

From Alabama to Wyoming, all states are pretty awesome. But Texas is different from all the rest—which you'll learn about in this here Texas history museum. Whether you're into shipwrecks or cowboys or outer space, the Lone Star State has had a hand in some pretty amazing events. And since it's way more fun to see, hear and touch than just read about something, the Bullock has lots of amazing things on display. Things like a real ship, called the *La Belle*, which sank near Galveston in 1664. They actually rebuilt it on the first floor of the building, and showcase things like muskets, beads, rings and knives that went down with the boat. They also have the actual Goddess of Liberty statue that sat on top of the Capitol for nearly 100 years, and a real mission control panel that NASA used to help astronauts make it to the moon.

FUN FACTS

» Bob Bullock was a powerful politician who loved history and worked to ensure the government established a museum that would tell the story of Texas.

» The Texan army was defeated at the Alamo by Mexican General Santa Anna's troops in 13 days. About six weeks later, the Texans beat that same army in just 18 minutes at the Battle of San Jacinto. (You can see an original painting of that scene if you visit the state Capitol!)

THE LOWDOWN

» TELL YOUR PARENTS   There is an IMAX Theater attached to the Bullock Museum that runs a mixture of current movies and documentaries. In the summer, there is a free family movie series. The Blanton Art Museum is right across the street, and the Texas Capitol is about four blocks in the other direction.

» KNOW BEFORE YOU GO   Located at 1800 N. Congress Ave., the Bullock Museum is open Monday through Saturday from 9AM to 5PM and Sundays from noon to 5PM. If you can't find street parking, there is a parking garage at 18th Street, on the south side of the museum that costs $8 for all day. Check thestoryoftexas.com for show times and other news. (512-936-8746)

DISCOVER MISSION #2   ON EVERY FLOOR OF THE MUSEUM, LEARN ABOUT (AT LEAST) ONE STORY YOU THINK IS INTERESTING. SAY TO YOUR PARENT OR FRIEND, "DID YOU KNOW…" AND TELL THEM YOUR TIDBIT FROM TEXAS HISTORY!

DISCOVER MISSION #3   WATCH THE VIDEO ABOUT LBJ'S DAUGHTERS ON THE 10TH FLOOR, AND THINK ABOUT WHAT IT MIGHT BE LIKE TO LIVE IN THE WHITE HOUSE WITH A SECRET SERVICE AGENT WATCHING OVER YOU. WOULD YOU TRY TO RUN AWAY?

LBJ PRESIDENTIAL LIBRARY

Do not go into this "library" expecting to check out the latest Rick Riordan book. Do go in expecting to see a limousine the size of a swimming pool, an ancient game of Twister, a short movie about kids who lived in the White House and a collection of papers that would pile (almost) as high as Mount Everest. Also, go in expecting to learn about Lyndon Baines Johnson, the 36th president of the United States, because every single thing in here is connected to his fascinating life. He lived from 1908 until 1973, and the history that unfolded during that time is pretty exciting. You will learn about Martin Luther King and civil rights, putting a man on the moon, and the Vietnam War. Even Sesame Street and the Beatles make their way into old LBJ's life.

 FUN FACTS

» LBJ was born in 1908. He grew up near Austin and was a schoolteacher before he entered politics.

» The museum contains 45 million pages of historical documents, 650,000 photos and 5,000 hours of recordings!

» The first presidential library was created for Herbert Hoover, the 31st president of the United States. Even though there have been 45 presidents, there are only 13 presidential libraries, so it's pretty neat that one is in Austin!

THE LOWDOWN

» TELL YOUR PARENTS The LBJ Library is on the University of Texas campus, so you can combine this visit with some other fun stops listed in the "Cool School" chapter of this book, like the nearby Texas Memorial Museum.

» KNOW BEFORE YOU GO The LBJ Library is located at 2313 Red River St. and is open from 9AM to 5PM every day. Admission is $8 for adults, $3 for kids 13-17 and free for children under 12. There is free parking in Lot 38 on Red River. For more information, visit lbjlibrary.org. (512-721-0200)

WRISTBANDS

HOT RODS HIT THE TRACK AND GO FAST,
MUSICIANS PLAY SONGS THAT YOU KNOW.
DANCE LIKE A WILD THING, WATCH CARS WHIZ PAST.
SMALL PAPER BRACELETS GET YOU INTO VERY BIG SHOWS!

WRISTBANDS MISSION #1   PART ONE: A WEEK BEFORE THE FESTIVAL, MAKE A FLAG (12 FEET TALL OR UNDER) TO CARRY AROUND SO EVERYONE IN YOUR GROUP WILL KNOW EXACTLY WHERE YOU ARE. PART TWO: WHEN YOU ARRIVE, TELL YOUR PARENTS WHERE TO MEET YOU IF THEY ACCIDENTALLY GET LOST.

AUSTIN CITY LIMITS MUSIC FESTIVAL

Did you know some people call Austin the "Live Music Capital of the World"? If you're lucky enough to go to the Austin City Limits Music Festival with your folks, you'll see why! Eight stages are set up all around Zilker Park, turning it into a crazy, fun, jam-packed, rocking extravaganza where you can listen to more than 100 bands. Unless you have magical winged shoes (or Hermione's time-turner) that can zip you around to see all the wonderful musicians, though, you'll have to choose some favorites. Because the whole festival is outside, you can boogie down, run and play as you listen, or sit and watch if you're in the mood to chill out. There's even a special area called "Austin Kiddie Limits," where you can pretend to be a rock star and do things like turn your hair orange, make videos and mustache masks, and play a real guitar. When you work up an appetite, visit the awesome food court and pick out something delicious to eat at the biggest, best, rock-and-rolliest picnic ever.

 FUN FACTS

» *Austin City Limits* is a TV show that started airing in 1974 (it might even be older than your parents). The first performer on the show was one of Austin's fave musicians, Willie Nelson.

» The festival started in 2002, and around 75,000 people attend each day. That's like dropping the population of a whole town into Zilker Park!

 THE LOWDOWN

» GEAR   Very comfy shoes, blankets or small folding chairs, sunscreen, water bottles or CamelBak, hacky sack or ball, stroller for legs that get tired easily.

» TELL YOUR PARENTS   Stop at the "Tag a Kid" station first! Come early and claim a shady spot to set up chairs and blankets. Look for free water stations throughout the park where you can refill bottles. Crowds get much bigger at the end of the day, and WiFi is spotty.

» KNOW BEFORE YOU GO   There are many pricing options for big kids and adults at aclfestival.com. Kids age 10 and under get in free!

SXSW (SOUTH BY SOUTHWEST)

It's kinda hard to explain exactly what SXSW is, but try to imagine a gigantic citywide music, movie and technology conference that grownups pay a lot of money to attend. ...Did you just make a yuck face and think, "Why would a KID want to go to THAT?" Well, think again, because there are lots of fun things for kids. If you're a music fan, there are free concerts all over town where really cool people play in cool places that you will think are FUN because they have playgrounds, lemonade, sidewalk chalk and lots of other kids! If you like video games, there is a huge SXSW Gaming Expo, where you might see demonstrations of new games, learn about the history of old ones and even compete against other kids in a tournament. There is also something called SXCreate, where you can see new technologies like 3D print-ers in action. There are events especially for kids like you, and others that are meant for kids of all ages, and you'll get to see funny stuff, like Willie Nelson mannequins.

FUN FACTS

» The first SXSW event was held in 1994, and 700 people attended. More than 100,000 attended in 2016, which means it's growing even faster than you!

THE LOWDOWN

» **GEAR**   Comfy shoes, cash for food vendors and musician tips, sunscreen, cool hat, water bottle.

» **TELL YOUR PARENTS**   There are some great resources to learn where and when kid-friendly events are being held. Check out livemom.com, freefuninaustin.com, do512family.com or 365thingsaustin.com for tips.

» **KNOW BEFORE YOU GO**   SXSW is held in venues all over town. Some tried-and-true daytime kid-friendly music venues include: Lucy's Fried Chicken, Whole Foods Market, Waterloo Records and wherever Sun Radio is hosting their morning and afternoon live broadcasts.

WRISTBANDS MISSION #2   BE A FRIEND TO A MUSICIAN, AND DROP AT LEAST $1 INTO A TIP JAR. BONUS POINTS IF YOU TAKE UP THE COLLECTION YOURSELF!

WRISTBANDS MISSION #3   MAKE UP A SPECIAL SLOGAN FOR THE CAR YOU HOPE
WINS THE RACE. EVERY TIME YOU SPOT IT COMING AROUND THE TRACK, YELL IT AT
THE TOP OF YOUR LUNGS AND PUNCH YOUR PARENT IN THE ARM (SOFTLY).

FORMULA ONE GRAND PRIX

Are you a kid who always picks the first seat on a roller coaster and loves to fly down steep hills on your bike? Are you known for knowing all about cars and for quoting along with the movie *Cars*? If so, you may have the NEED FOR SPEED, and will love going to see the only Formula One car race in the entire country. But, even if you like lightning bugs more than Lightning McQueen, you can still have fun at the Circuit of the Americas racetrack, because there is always a huge concert, and some fun kid-friendly activities.

Come up with a team name, and design your own super-rad racecar.

 FUN FACTS

» "Formula" refers to the set of rules drivers and their teams have to follow; "one" means it is the top racing category.

» The 3.4-mile-long Circuit of the Americas track was built especially for Formula 1 racing, and drivers have to go around it 56 times.

» These cars can go more than 200 miles per hour!

» "Grand Prix" is French for "big prize."

 THE LOWDOWN

» GEAR   Blanket or chairs (if you have general admission tickets), a backpack with sealed water bottles, sunglasses, hat, earplugs, poncho or small umbrella.

» TELL YOUR PARENTS   Coolers aren't allowed, so be prepared to buy food onsite.

» KNOW BEFORE YOU GO   The track is located about 25 minutes from downtown Austin at 9201 Circuit of the Americas Blvd. Shuttles are available, so check circuitoftheamericas.com for details.

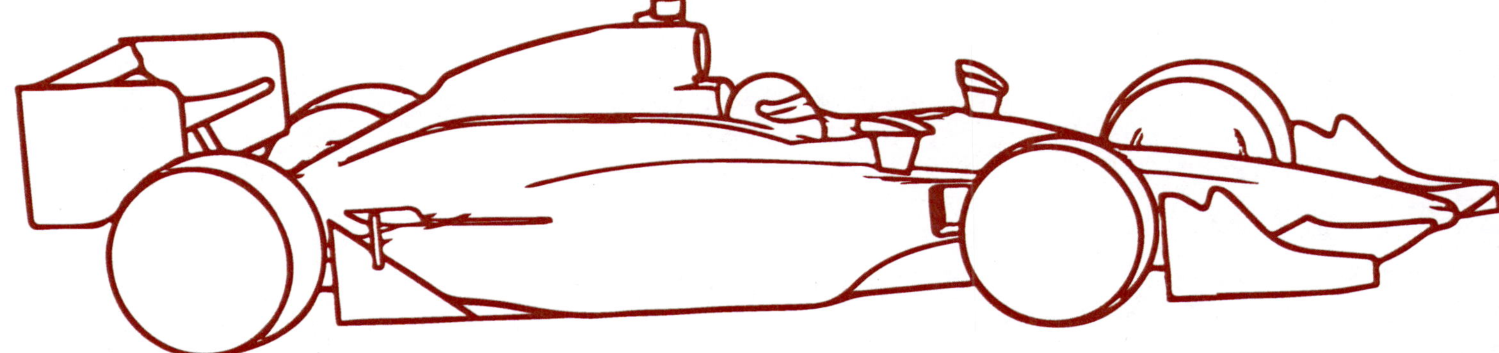

amy's
ICE CREAM

MUNCH

A KID'S GOTTA EAT, SO GO ON AND DAYDREAM
'BOUT PIZZA AND PANCAKES ON A PLATE OF YOUR OWN.
BURGERS AND TACOS, SNOW CONES AND ICE CREAM...
SOME THINGS ARE YUMMY, EVEN WHEN YOU'RE QUITE GROWN.

MUNCH MISSION #1 WALK UP TO THE COUNTER AND PLACE AND PAY FOR YOUR FAMILY'S ORDER ALL BY YOURSELF. TELL THE PERSON BEHIND THE COUNTER, "THANKS. KEEP IT WEIRD, DUDE!"

P. TERRY'S BURGER STAND

There are lots of fast-food burger places on the planet, but there can only be *one* best fast-food burger place on the planet. If Austin got to decide, the "best" award would probably go to P. Terry's. It's hard to explain exactly why it's the treat you want after a soccer game, on a busy weeknight and when your mom brings a special lunch to school. But, it is what you'll want to have on lots of those occasions. Sometimes, it's hard to beat a good burger, fries and a milkshake!

🍴 FUN FACTS

» Americans eat nearly 50 billion burgers a year! That is 50,000,000,000!

» P. Terry's was started in Austin in 2005 by two very nice people named Patrick and Kathy Terry. They do their best to use healthy ingredients and treat their employees well, and they give a lot of money back to the community.

» All P. Terry's restaurants are designed using the Googie style of architecture, so they might remind you of a space ship or old-fashioned drive-in.

THE LOWDOWN

» TELL YOUR PARENTS   You can order all kinds of sandwiches from P. Terry's, like chicken burgers, veggie burgers and gluten-free lettuce wraps. They also have delicious milkshakes and banana bread for breakfast.

» KNOW BEFORE YOU GO   There are lots of P. Terry's locations scattered around town, but the original is on the corner of Barton Springs Rd. and Lamar Blvd. Most open for breakfast at 7AM or 8AM and serve food until very, very late. Check pterrys.com for specifics.

HOME SLICE PIZZA

Pizza goes with ping pong like donuts go with sleepovers. At least it does at Austin's Home Slice Pizza—which means it's fun to wait for a table at this popular restaurant right in the middle of a busy stretch of South Congress Avenue. Table tennis isn't the only reason to come here, though, because the pizza is dee-licious! The slices are HUGE, and you're actually supposed to fold them up into a funny kind of edible origami. Check out the menu for directions, and do your best to have a very messy face after each bite.

FUN FACTS

» Home Slice serves a crispy-crusted New York-style pizza, which is based on "Neapolitan" pies from Naples, Italy.

» Pizza-making is taken very seriously in Italy, and restaurants can only call their pies "Neapolitan" if they follow strict guidelines about how the dough is made, the kind of oven they use, and what kind of cheese goes on top.

» Home Slice was created by three good friends, Terri Hannefin, Joseph Strickland and "Queen of Pies" Jen Strickland, who developed the restaurant's recipe. They take pizza-making seriously, too, and do lots of nice things for the Austin community.

THE LOWDOWN

» **TELL YOUR PARENTS** If you're still hungry after eating pizza and salad, you can get a cone full of something cold and dreamy at the Amy's Ice Cream location just a few blocks south.

» **KNOW BEFORE YOU GO** Located at 1415 S. Congress Ave., Home Slice is closed Tuesdays but open from 11AM to 11PM most nights, and until midnight on weekends. There is designated parking in a church lot on Elizabeth St. They don't deliver, but the More Home Slice take-out location right next door is open every day of the week. See what's happening at homeslicepizza.com—maybe you'll be lucky and catch some live music or the Carnival O' Pizza! (512-444-PIES)

MUNCH MISSION #2   CHALLENGE SOMEONE TO A GAME OF PING PONG. WHOEVER WINS GETS TO CHOOSE PIZZA TOPPINGS, BUT THE LOSER GETS THE FIRST PIECE.

MUNCH MISSION #3 LOOK AROUND THE FOOD TRUCK PARK AND COUNT HOW MANY CULTURES ARE REPRESENTED IN THE FOOD. WHEN YOU ORDER, CHOOSE SOMETHING YOU'VE NEVER TRIED!

FOOD COURT TRAILER PARKS

Options are always good, but especially at dinnertime. That's why if you like a food buffet, you will LOVE Austin's food court trailer parks. Let's say you want soup but your sister wants a rice bowl. Or your Mom wants salad and your Dad wants tacos. Well, you can either drive around playing Rock-Paper-Scissors and see who wins, or go to a food truck trailer park and everyone can have exactly what they want. Outside. At a picnic table. Without a single backseat loser pouting through the meal.

Design your own food truck and come up with a funny name for your new business.

 **FUN FACTS**

» There are more than 1,000 food trailers in Austin.

» Lots of delicious local restaurants started out as food trailers. You might try Torchy's Tacos if you love queso, or the Peached Tortilla if you like Asian food.

 **THE LOWDOWN**

» **TELL YOUR PARENTS** There are food trailer parks all over Austin, including lots of options at The Picnic and Midway Food Park. The Midway has live music and a great playground; The Picnic has shade, clean bathrooms and a great location near Lady Bird Lake. You can search for trailers by location at foodtrailersaustin.com.

» **KNOW BEFORE YOU GO** The Picnic is located at 1720 Barton Springs Rd. (thepicnicaustin.com) and Midway Food Park is at 1905 S. Capital of Texas Highway (themidwayfoodpark.com). Some food trucks only take cash.

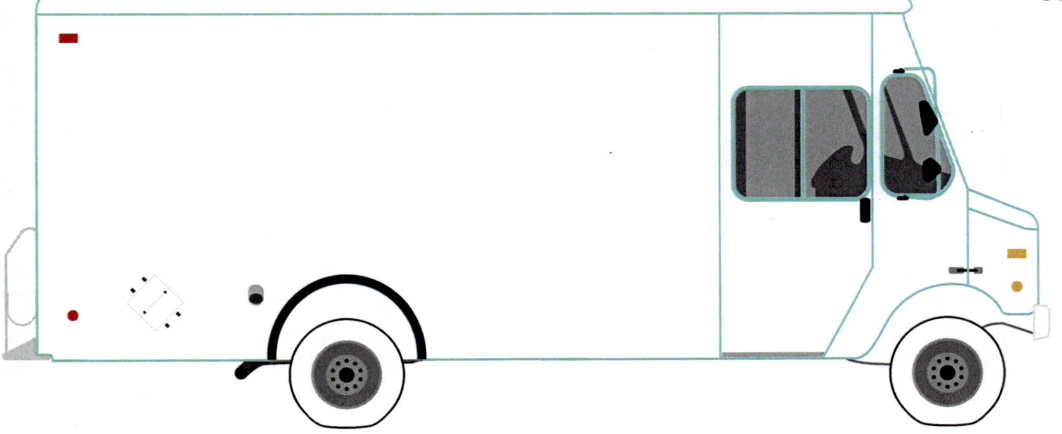

COOL SCHOOL

THE UNIVERSITY OF TEXAS IS SIMPLY NOT SMALL,
SO THERE'S ROOM FOR ALL THOUGHTS AND ALL KINDS.
PAINTINGS AND DINOS, BOOKS AND FOOTBALL,
CHOICES GALORE FOR SMART KIDDO MINDS.

COOL SCHOOL MISSION #1   LOCATE EL ANATSUI'S SCULPTURE, "SEEPAGE." FIND OUT WHAT IT IS MADE OF, AND THINK OF SOMETHING YOU COULD MAKE FROM THE SAME FOUND OBJECTS. TELL A GROWNUP WHY YOU DO OR DO NOT LIKE IT.

BLANTON MUSEUM OF ART

This may be the only museum in the world where you can go for a swim…if you use your imagination. That's because you walk right into a giant blue sculpture that looks like the deep end of a shimmering swimming pool. There are lots of other nifty things to see after you pretend-backstroke your way upstairs. Be on the lookout for immortals you might read about in a Percy Jackson book, and see who can be the quietest in a room filled with gazillions of pennies. In addition to touring the museum, you might have an opportunity to make a masterpiece of your own or learn about something special during a family day. In the summertime, you won't believe your eyes when you see all of the crazy, fun, free art supplies you can use in the Blanton's WorkLAB. It's a workstation that will give your imagination the inspiration it needs to make a magnificent creation. No exaggeration!

FUN FACTS

» Artist Teresita Fernández calls her blue pool *Stacked Waters*, and says she wants you to feel like you are part of the sculpture.

» The Blanton has more than 18,000 works of art. You can't see them all in the museum at one time, but you can see them online!

THE LOWDOWN

» TELL YOUR PARENTS   In the summer, be sure and check out WorkLAB, Artists and Authors or Deeper Dives for some hands-on fun. If you get hungry, there is a terrific café just across the courtyard from the museum.

» KNOW BEFORE YOU GO   The Blanton is open from 10AM to 5PM Tuesday through Friday, 11AM to 5PM on Saturday and 1PM to 5PM on Sunday. Admission is $9 for adults, $5 for kids over 13 and free for kids 12 and under. Third Thursdays are free. The museum is located at 200 E. Martin Luther King Jr. Blvd. and parking is available in the garage on the corner of Brazos and MLK for $4 with museum validation. Check blantonmuseum.org to see if there are some special kid programs when you visit. (512-471-7324)

TEXAS MEMORIAL MUSEUM

A better name for this place might be "Mad Scientist's Laboratory Full of Dinosaur Bones, Fancy Rocks, Cool Critters and Genius Stuff," because it's way more fun than the official name sounds. Depending on how you feel about dinosaurs, you will either be amazed or terrified by skeletons of a huge Texas Pterosaur and 30-foot long Onion Creek Mosasaur. You will want to take home the beautiful, sparkly and humongous gemstones and meteorites and put them in your backyard. (Don't do it! You'll get in trouble!) Also, the Hall of Texas Wildlife is filled with real animal specimens to show you life in Texas habitats. Finally, the top floor has lots of cool models and interactive displays that show off the experiments of real scientists. One of the coolest lets you look in a mirror and see how closely related humans are to chimpanzees. Just because you look like one doesn't mean you should act like one, though.

Fill in these picture frames with drawings of Texas wildlife you see in the museum.

FUN FACTS

» Mosasaurs lived right here in the Austin area but have been extinct for 66 million years.

» Topaz is the state gemstone of Texas.

» The Texas Pterosaur is the largest flying reptile ever discovered!

THE LOWDOWN

» **TELL YOUR PARENTS** If you want to see more of campus after your visit, bring snacks and water, and do some of the Landmarks walking tour (landmarks.utexas.edu/visit). The closest is Tony Smith's *Amaryllis sculpture*, located at the Fine Arts Complex.

» **KNOW BEFORE YOU GO** Located at 2400 Trinity St., the museum is open from 9AM to 5PM Tuesday through Saturday. Parking is available in the San Jacinto Garage at 2500 San Jacinto Blvd. ($3 per hour). Entry is $3 for kids 12 and under, and $4 for everyone else. Visit tmm.utexas.edu for more information. (512-471-1604)

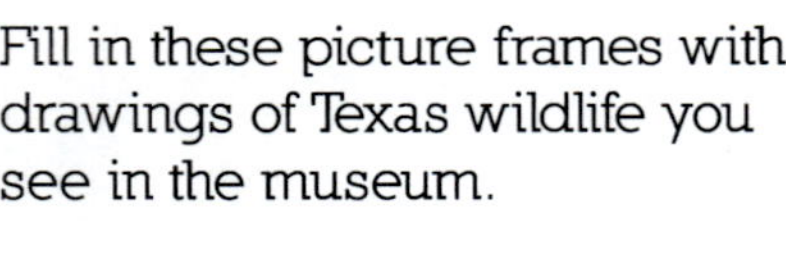

COOL SCHOOL MISSION #2   WHEN YOU GET TO THE HALL OF TEXAS WILDLIFE, FIND THE AUDIO TOUR QUESTION THAT ASKS, "HOW DID THE MUSEUM GET THESE ANIMALS?" CALL THE NUMBER AND FIND OUT!

COOL SCHOOL MISSION #3   AT LEAST ONCE DURING THE GAME, MAKE THE "HOOK 'EM HORNS" HAND SIGNAL (EVEN IF YOU'RE ROOTING FOR THE OTHER TEAM AND TURN IT UPSIDE DOWN.)

LONGHORN FOOTBALL GAME

Hook 'em Horns! One of the funny things about a college football game is that you don't even have to like sports to enjoy it. That's because, in addition to the throws, punts, tackles and touch-downs happening on the field, there are cheerleaders, dance teams, marching bands and mascots putting on another show in the stands and on the sidelines. Keep an eye out for The University of Texas mascot, Bevo—he'll be the 2,000-pound, four-footed, long-horned guy down in the end zone. It's also awesome to be in the Darrell K. Royal Stadium because, like lots of things in Texas, it is HUGE! So huge, in fact, that 100,000 people can be inside at once (betcha can't count 'em all).

FUN FACTS

» Darrell K. Royal coached the Texas Longhorn football team for 21 years and won three national championships.

» UT's school colors made their first appearance in 1885 after two Longhorn fans stopped to get ribbons for the crowd on the way to a baseball game, and the store had more orange and white than any other colors.

» There are a lot of theories about how Bevo got his name. One possibility is that it is a play on "beeves," the plural word for "beef."

THE LOWDOWN

» GEAR   Burnt orange clothing (if you're a Longhorn fan, that is), sunscreen in warm months, blanket in cool months, chair backs or seat cushions.

» TELL YOUR PARENTS   You want to come early and see some of the pre-game shenanigans! If you can't make it to a game, but would like a stadium tour, visit utexas.edu/visitor-resources for more information.

» KNOW BEFORE YOU GO   You are not allowed to bring in food and drink, but there are plenty of fast-food and typical concession options. On game day, parking is tough in nearby garages, but there are shuttles to and from campus. Take a look at the Football Fan Guice on texassports.com for more information about game day.

THE SCOOP...

A BATTY LITTLE BOOKLET
FULL OF AUSTINTATIOUS EXTRAS
LIKE A CALENDAR OF EVENTS,
GROOVY GAMES AND
MORE POPULAR PLACES.

MARK YOUR CALENDARS!

All the stuff you won't want to miss

JANUARY

Martin Luther King Festival

Ice Skating on the Plaza at
Whole Foods Headquarters

FEBRUARY

Girls in Engineering Day at UT-Austin

MARCH

Explore UT-Austin

Zilker Kite Festival

Rodeo Austin

SXSW

Austin Parks Foundation (APF) Movies
in the Park Series

APRIL

Eeyore's Birthday Party

Old Settler's Music Festival

APF Movies in the Park Series

MAY

Pecan Street Spring Arts Festival

Woodland Faerie Trail at Zilker Botanical Garden

Blues on the Green

APF Movies in the Park Series

Kerrville Folk Festival

JUNE

Kids Camp at Alamo Movie Theaters

Deep Eddy Splash Party Movie Nights

Woodland Faerie Trail at Zilker Botanical Garden

Free Family Movie Series at the Bullock Museum

Summer Family Programs at the Blanton

Blues on the Green

Nature Nights at the
Ladybird Johnson Wildflower Center

Austin Symphony Concerts in the Park
at the Long Center

Unplugged at the Grove

JULY

Kids Camp at Alamo Movie Theaters

Deep Eddy Splash Party Movie Nights

Free Family Movie Series at the Bullock Museum

Zilker Hillside Theater Summer Musical

Fourth of July Fireworks and Symphony

Summer Family Programs at the Blanton

Blues on the Green

Austin Symphony Concerts in the Park
at the Long Center

Unplugged at the Grove

AUGUST

Kids Camp at Alamo Movie Theaters

Deep Eddy Splash Party Movie Nights

Free Family Movie Series at the Bullock Museum

Austin Ice Cream Festival

Summer Family Programs at the Blanton

Blues on the Green

Austin Symphony Concerts in the Park
at the Long Center

Unplugged at the Grove

SEPTEMBER

ACL Festival

The Old Pecan Street Festival

OCTOBER

ACL Festival

Dia de los Muertos Festival

Formula One United States Grand Prix

NOVEMBER

Fossil Fest

Texas Book Festival

DECEMBER

Austin Trail of Lights

Zilker Holiday Tree Lighting

Luminations at the Wildflower Center

Holiday Singalong and Downtown Stroll

Ballet Austin's Nutcracker

SO. MANY. PLACES.

Want the Expedition to continue? Check out even more fun Austin top spots!

SPLASH

Bartholomew Pool

PADDLE & RIDE

The Veloway
Bull Creek

SHOP

Anna's Toy Depot
Terra Toys
Tyler Sports
Half Price Books
Whole Earth Provisions

MUNCH

Torchy's Tacos
Guero's
Central Market
Whole Foods downtown

GOOF OFF

Central Market Playground
Crux Climbing Center
Austin Bouldering Project

ROAD TRIP

Pedernales Falls
Hamilton Pool Preserve
Johnson City

 ## EXPLORE

Austin Zoo
McKinney Falls State Park
Mount Bonnell

 ## WONDER

The Contemporary Austin
Mexic-Arte Museum

 ## BIG NIGHT OUT

Scottish Rite Children's Theater
Fresa's Chicken al Carbon
(South 1st location)
Threadgill's World Headquarters

 ## WRISTBANDS

Old Settler's Music Festival
Kerrville Folk Festival

DISCOVER 

Camp Mabry
Splash! Barton Springs Exhibit
George Washington Carver Museum
& Multicultural Center
The Thinkery

 ## COOL SCHOOL

The University of Texas Tower Tour

LET'S PLAY QUIZ

You've read, you've learned, you've seen, you've done—
now show off what you know!

1. How cold is Barton Springs? _______________________

2. Who was Ann Richards? (circle one)
    A. The first elected female governor of Texas
    B. A famous blues guitarist
    C. A local BMX bike rider

3. What is the name of the Texas prize for children's literature?
    ____

4. What city and country gave the world Neapolitan pizza crust?
    ____

5. What does the acronym "ROY G BIV" stand for (hint: all the visible colors on the light spectrum)?
    ____

6. What kind of rock formation is
    Enchanted Rock?
    (circle one)
    A. A butte
    B. A batholith
    C. An escarpment

7. How many tons of junk are built into the Cathedral of Junk? _______________________________

8. What is the largest flying creature ever discovered? _________________________________

9. When was the first coin-operated pinball machine developed? _____________________________

10. ___________ people attended the first SXSW event in 1994. More than ___________ attended in 2016.

11. Who was the Alamo hero who was known for wearing a coonskin cap? (circle one)
    A. Stephen F. Austin
    B. David Crockett
    C. Lyndon Baines Johnson

12. What is an aqueduct? ____
    ____

ANSWERS: 1. 68 degrees 2. A 3. Bluebonnet Award
4. Naples, Italy 5. Red, orange, yellow, green, blue, indigo
and violet 6. B 7. 60 tons 8. Texas Pterosaur
9. The 1930s 10. 700; 100,000 11. B 12. A manmade
channel for carrying water

📷 PHOTO SCAVENGER HUNT

Find these Austin icons in the real world, take a photo and ask a grownup to post them to Instagram using #ExpeditionAustin. Email info@expeditionaustin.com when you've posted all 20 to receive a special reward.

Barton Creek
Greenbelt
1010 Home Dale Barton Hills Access

PETER PAN
MINI GOLF

Book Kids

AMO
TICKETS

WIMB
BLUE
REGIONA

ACKNOWLEDGMENTS

We are grateful to so many people for their support in bringing *Expedition Austin* to life! First, we want to thank our families for listening to countless hours of book chatter, agreeing to relentless requests for input, and participating in mostly-awesome-but-sometimes-not research.

In addition, we are indebted to many smart, generous people for sharing their skills and expertise: Amy Spiro for her insightful feedback, Debra Farris for eagle eye copyediting, Travis Habersaat for allowing us to use his architectural rendering of the Cathedral of Junk, Dean Rader for keeping us on the copyright straight and narrow, Jessie La Patra Greene for her thoughtful suggestions, Wade Coody for nitpicking and Jamie Allen for brainstorming on the front end. We owe you all a book and a beer.

We also want to give a resounding shout of thanks to Austin's graffiti artists, muralists, business owners, preservationists, musicians, forward thinkers, and creative spirits for making our town awesome.

Last but not least, Jill's gratitude to her parents goes way, way back, because she originally came to Austin as a Longhorn on their dime.

PHOTO CREDITS

Austin and its gorgeous children are the stars of our book, and we are thankful to so many friends for loaning us their little supermodels, as well as to the following parents for sharing their fab photos with us: Nicole Basham (cover image), Amy Campbell (title page), Barbara LeGere (barbaralegerephotography.com; pages 72 and 87), Susan Brennan (page 6), Monica Maldonado Williams (pages 13 and 52), Katie Henry (pages 24 and 77), Ryan Allen (page 27), Jamie Allen (pages 35 and 48), Kirk Gillette (page 81), Steven Bijl (page 90) and Matthew Wheeler (pages 106 and 107).

ABOUT THE AUTHOR & ILLUSTRATOR/DESIGNER

After nearly 20 years in Austin, Jill Coody Smits is still in love with this little big town. She is a freelance writer of many things, including articles, blog posts, op-eds and essays published in outlets like Psychology Today, Spirit Magazine, Southern Living, Austin Monthly, Design*Sponge, the Washington Post, and CNN.com. She lives in south Austin with her husband, daughter and two four-footed sons. Follow Jill's other pursuits at **blueseedcommunications.com** as well as on Instagram (@ExpeditionAustin) and Twitter (@JCoodySmits).

Virginia Shurgar Hassell has spent years honing her skills at various creative agencies and in publishing, and as the owner of BigStar Creative. Her creative inspiration for this book comes from the vibrant, expressive nature of Austin and the people that keep it so wonderfully weird. She can be found just west of Austin with her sweet children, husband and the Texas hills. Virginia can be found on **bigstarcreative.com**, Twitter (@BigStarCreative) and Instagram (@virginiashassell).

CONTINUE THE EXPEDITION!

VISIT EXPEDITIONAUSTIN.COM OR FOLLOW THE TRAIL ON INSTAGRAM  @EXPEDITIONAUSTIN AND #EXPEDITIONAUSTIN